THEN & NOW

BUTTE

Opposite: The seven stacks of the Neversweat Mine are iconic in historic photographs portraying Butte's greatest nickname, "The Richest Hill on Earth." Situated on the east side of the hill, the Neversweat (left) and adjacent Anaconda, owned by copper king Marcus Daly, were two important mines that helped Butte emerge from a small mining camp into one of the world's greatest copper producers. (Courtesy of Butte-Silver Bow Archives.)

THEN & NOW

BUTTE

Matt Vincent and Chad Okrusch

This book is dedicated to Butte native and community leader, George Paul. A staunch supporter of the city's past, present, and future, "Georgie" was a shining example of the fiercely loyal and charismatic people who make Butte, as much as its mineral wealth, "The Richest Hill on Earth."

ISBN 978-0-7385-8182-8

Library of Congress Control Number: 2010936335

Published by Arcadia Publishing
Charleston, South Carolina

Printed in the United States of America

For all general information, please contact Arcadia Publishing:
Telephone 843-853-2070
Fax 843-853-0044
E-mail sales@arcadiapublishing.com
For customer service and orders:
Toll-Free 1-888-313-2665

Visit us on the Internet at www.arcadiapublishing.com

On the Front Cover: The tall, iron structures prominently dotting Butte's landscape are called headframes. Miners referred to them, both figuratively and literally, as "gallows frames." In nearly a century of underground mining operations, over 2,500 men died beneath Butte. The Bell-Diamond is pictured here overlooking the city from the east. Its toxic dumps were remediated, including construction of a walking trail in 2009. (Then image courtesy of BSB Archives.)

On the Back Cover: St. John's Episcopal Church was originally built in 1881 on the southwest corner of Idaho and Broadway Streets. A fire destroyed the structure in 1919, and it was rebuilt using granite from one of Butte's many local quarries in classic Norman architectural style in 1921. This photograph was taken prior to the fire around 1900. (Courtesy of BSB Archives.)

Contents

ACKNOWLEDGMENTS

We would like to thank the following people and organizations: Ellen Crain and Lee Whitney at the Butte-Silver Bow Public Archives; World Museum of Mining's Tina Greene, Delores Cooney, and Jim Killoy; Keith Blount; Bob Liva; John T., Evelyn, and Gerri Shea; Danny Tam Wong, Sharon Tam, and Jerry Tam of the Pekin Noodle Parlor; Quarry Brewery owners Chuck and Lyza Schnabel; Ray Ueland at the Metals Bank; Bob Lazetich and the Butte Country Club; Kathy Finch at Second Edition Books; Marko Lucich with the Butte Chamber of Commerce; Sara Sparks of the Environmental Protection Agency's Butte Office; Marci Sheehan at Atlantic Richfield Corporation; the Clark Fork Watershed Education Program and Technical Communications Department at Montana Tech; and Chris Fisk, Paul Tash, and Marcia Lubick at Montana Tech Library Archives. Without their generosity, hospitality, and assistance, this book would not have been possible. The majority of the earlier photographs are courtesy of the Butte-Silver Bow Public Archives (BSB Archives), World Museum of Mining, and the Library of Congress Prints and Photographs Online Catalog. Keith Blount created the Butte then and now map. All now images were taken by Matt Vincent and Chad Okrusch.

We would also like to thank our editor at Arcadia, John Poultney, for his guidance and patience throughout the project. Lastly and most importantly, we express our deepest love and gratitude to our wives, Alicia (Vincent) and Margi (Okrusch), for their support, patience, and understanding.

A portion of the proceeds from this book will be donated by the authors to support the Clark Fork Watershed Education Program and the Technical Communications Department at Montana Tech.

Introduction

A long-standing highway sign tells Butte's past fairly accurately and succinctly:

> Butte owes its existence to placer gold discovered on Silver Bow Creek in 1864, but the gold soon played out and it was demand for Butte's copper that made it "the richest hill on Earth." The hill produced over two billion dollars worth of gold, silver, copper and zinc. Drifts, winzes and stopes honeycombed the underground, creating a labyrinth that still extends beneath the city. There were over 3,000 miles of workings, and shafts some reaching a depth of 4,000 feet. In 1955, the Anaconda Company opened the Berkeley Pit to mine low-grade metals. The pit swallowed up Meaderville, McQueen and copper king W.A. Clark's famed Columbia Gardens amusement park.
>
> Butte has a cosmopolitan population derived from the four corners of the world. She was a bold, unashamed rootin', tootin' hell-roarin' camp in days gone by and still drinks her liquor straight.
>
> At the heart of American unionism with a labor history second to none in the nation, the National Park Service recognized Butte as a National Historic Landmark (NHL) in 1961.

Timing and location are both critical keys to success. Butte's prominence as a mining camp of global significance and its uniqueness as a one-of-a-kind community are perfect case studies. Discovery of one of the earth's greatest deposits of copper coincided with the dawn of the electrical industrial age, creating an insatiable demand for Butte's inexhaustible supply. This in turn initiated a necessity for labor and services that came along at precisely the same time as America's immigration peak. Thousands of Europeans, Asians, and others coming to America in search of an opportunity for a better life were offered a veritable guarantee in Butte. The fertile grounds of Butte's mineral wealth, cultivated by hard-working new Americans, produced a harvest that was reaped from coast to coast and beyond.

Fellow Butte authors Ellen Crain and Lee Whitney in Images of America: *Butte* described the city according to a 1905 story in the *Butte Evening Post* as "cosmopolitan, strenuous, unique, and prosperous." It is perhaps these qualities that cause Butte's proud citizens to speak of their hometown in superlatives and lavish nicknames. The Richest Hill on Earth, The City of Champions, Butte America, are just a few of the titles to which Butte lays claim unabashedly. The best explanation for this pride is that all of the names are true, at least in greater part if not only figuratively. It is the pride and loyalty of Butte's own who have kept it a place worthy of such.

"There's only one place in the world called Butte, Montana," says former miner John T. Shea, whose family came from County Cork, Ireland, to "the Mining City" in the late 1800s. "People stuck together and stayed behind each other no matter what. It was a melting pot: there were Italians, Irish, Cornish and Bohunks. They were their nationality, but then they were Butte."

Butte has endured and even enjoyed a roller coaster ride of ups and downs since its founding over 150 years ago. There have been hundreds of books, both fiction and factual, written about the town and people, their trials, and tribulations. Even so, there are a million stories more, proudly passed on and around by the folks whose families have called Butte home for generations. This book cannot even scratch the surface of Butte's depth, which extends far beyond its great pit or deepest mine, but it is a telling introduction of what the town beholds beneath its gritty appearance. Despite all that has been published, there has never been a volume that attempts to compare Butte exclusively in its "then and now." Hopefully readers will find it interesting and find new ways to appreciate a town to which our nation owes its deepest gratitude.

CHAPTER 1

THE NATURAL AND BUILT ENVIRONMENT

Butte lies on the western face of the Continental Divide, which surrounds the town in a semicircle. The Lady of the Rockies is a 90-foot-tall statue of the Virgin Mary, erected by former miners in 1986 atop the divide's 8,500-foot-high East Ridge. Butte's existence is a credit to the mutual forces of man and earth.

The Big Butte, an igneous formation 6,310 feet above the west side of the valley, gave Butte (formerly Butte City) its name. In 1910, students from the Montana School of Mines (now Montana Tech) constructed the "M" out of whitewashed rhyolite. Each July 3, the Big Butte serves as the launch site for the city's Independence Day fireworks display, a celebration worthy of spectacle. The "M" is visible throughout the city, as seen here from a Virginia Street location. (Then photograph courtesy of BSB Archives.)

Silver Bow Creek drains Butte's Summit Valley and is the northeastern headwaters of the Columbia River. The first maps of the area from the 1870s show the creek already heavily diverted to mining mills, concentrating plants, and tailings ponds. Many locals know the stream as Copper Creek, Metro Storm Drain, and Shit Creek. After over a century of use as a municipal and industrial sewer, Silver Bow Creek is slowly being restored to a functioning stream again. (Then photograph courtesy of World Museum of Mining.)

Butte's intense mining resulted almost immediately in the depletion and contamination of local waters. Heavy metals and acidic mining runoff required Butte to look to its outlying areas for clean sources. Across the Continental Divide to the East, the Big Hole River is located 25 miles south of town and provides most (around 60 percent) of the city supply. Built in the 1890s, the Big Hole system is currently being updated, as local water is still unfit for potable use. (Then photograph courtesy of BSB Archives.)

Constructed in the late 1880s, the Basin Creek Reservoir system supplies around 30 percent of the city's water. Even though most of Butte's immediate water is contaminated, the Basin Creek supply located in the Highlands Mountains 15 miles to the south is a testament to some of the more pristine surrounding environs. An old rock dam was in need of improvements in 2009, but water is still pure enough that it does not need to be filtered. (Then photograph courtesy of BSB Archives.)

When Butte constructed its city water supply and transmission system in the late 1880s/early 1900s, the technology and equipment available were primitive compared to today's standards. Construction of dams and subterranean water lines were early engineering marvels of America's West, completed mostly by manpower and digging by hand. This photograph set compares the Big Hole transmission line as it was installed around 1900 and its ongoing replacement, which began in 2009. (Then photograph courtesy of BSB Archives.)

Butte's industrial past did not allow much of anything to grow on its steep, rocky slopes. Rain and melting snow ran downhill with great speed and force, which required their flows to be directed away from mines and residences. Missoula Gulch, pictured here, is the largest drainage on the hill. Sections of the 1940s-constructed storm sewer are over 30-feet subsurface, another early feat of construction and engineering. Shallow sections of the line were partially reconstructed in the late 1990s. (Then photograph courtesy of World Museum of Mining.)

Lake Avoca was created in the early 1900s by damming Blacktail Creek, located out on the flats of Butte. The dam was breached, and the lake was drained in 1935 to provide expansion of the Butte Country Club into an 18-hole course, one of Montana's oldest. This view is on the 13th-hole fairway. Street names in the area, such as North Lake and East Lake Drives, give hints of the former lake setting. (Then photograph courtesy of the Butte Country Club.)

Highway 2 climbs circuitously across the Continental Divide south of Butte and summits at just under 7,000 feet. Still known to locals as "Harding Way" (named after former U.S. president Warren G. Harding), the route offers a close-up look at numerous granitic outcrops of the Boulder batholith, the geologic phenomenon responsible for Butte's vast mineral wealth. Rich veins of metal-bearing minerals filled cracks in the granite as it cooled 75 million years ago. (Then photograph courtesy of BSB Archives.)

This 1875 photograph shows Butte City as a mining camp with only a few thousand residents. Silver kept Butte from becoming another western mining ghost town, but it was copper king Marcus Daly's discovery of rich copper in his Anaconda Mine in 1881 that turned Butte into a bustling metropolis. Today the city has 35,000 residents and a diversified economy. The only mine (Montana Resources) still operating is an open pit copper/molybdenum operation that employs 300. (Then photograph courtesy of World Museum of Mining.)

CHAPTER 2

THE MINING CITY

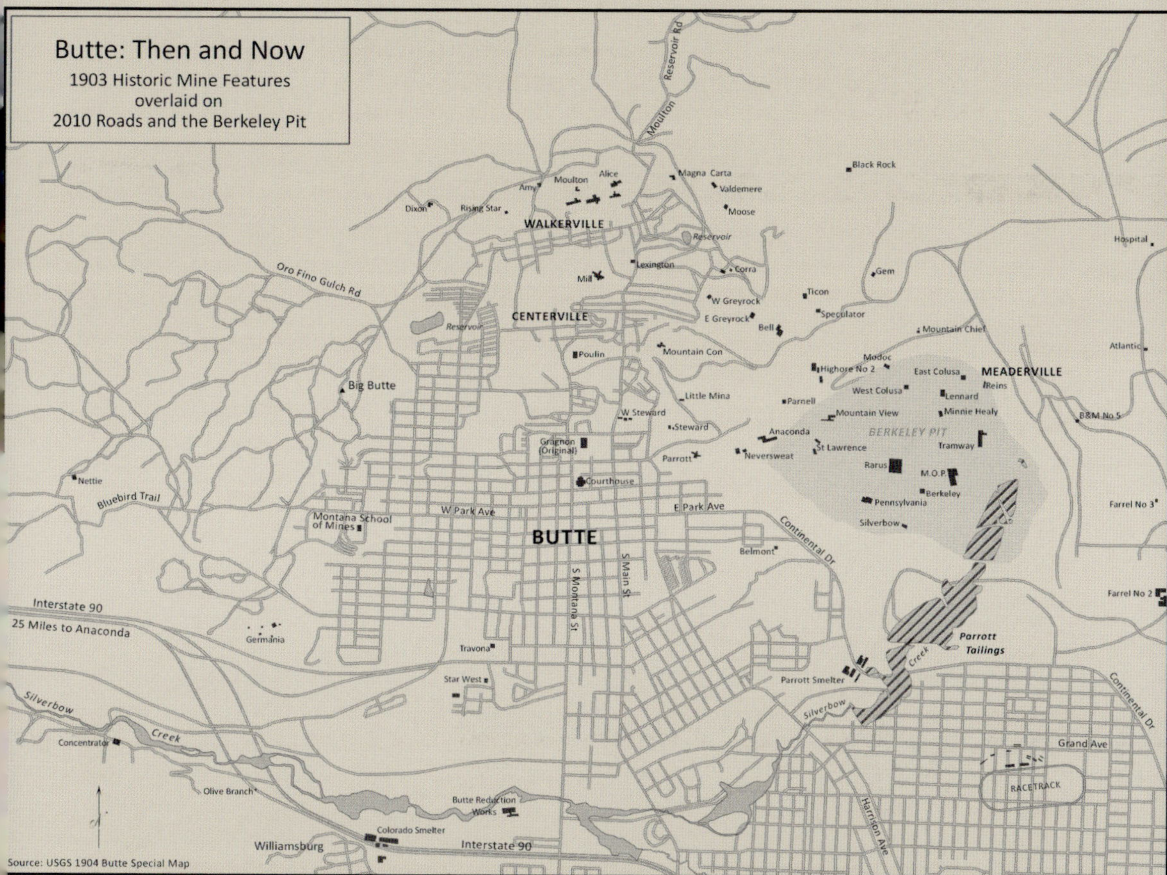

This map shows Butte as it existed in 1903, overlaid upon a 2010 city streets map. The Mining City (Butte) and the Smelter City (Anaconda) boasted a combined population well over 100,000, according to the 1920 census. Much has changed. Of particular interest, notice how much of Butte's east side was consumed by the Berkeley Pit. (Map created by Keith Blount.)

Butte started its existence like every other mining camp of the mid-1800s: as a placer gold discovery. Barker and Party found gold in Silver Bow Creek in the fall of 1864 near the present-day burg of Silver Bow. In 1929, a marker was placed at the discovery site by the Butte Daughters of the American Revolution. The original bronze plaque was stolen in the 1950s; the sign was replaced with a polished granite marker in 2008. (Then photograph courtesy of BSB Archives.)

After miners dredged the gold out of Silver Bow Creek, they turned their attention upstream to the rich veins of silver and copper beneath Butte's hill. Early underground mines, such as the Orphan Boy (pictured here around 1900) had their timber hoists housed within large buildings. When mines reached more significant depths, the head frames became the towering iron structures as seen on this book's cover. Remnants of the Orphan Boy are located just west of the World Museum of Mining. (Then photograph courtesy of BSB Archives.)

Incorporated in 1890 and named after prominent Salt Lake City brothers who owned a number of silver mines, Walkerville is Butte's northern suburb. Its most important historical role is that the Walkers brought copper king Marcus Daly to Butte in 1876 to help expand their Alice Mine and Mill. While working for the Walkers, Daly did his own prospecting and found vast copper underground in the Anaconda mine. The large mine dumps in this early 1980s photograph are reclaimed now. (Then photograph courtesy of EPA.)

Marcus Daly was one of Butte's three "copper kings" and the founder and mastermind behind the Anaconda Company and city of Anaconda. A bronze statue of his likeness was unveiled in front of the federal courthouse on North Main Street in 1906. The statue was moved to the campus of Montana Tech in the 1930s, where it still stands today. From his current Park Street perch, he can rightly overlook the city he helped build. (Then photograph courtesy of BSB Archives.)

The Montana School of Mines was founded in 1900. This photograph was taken shortly after the gymnasium building (on the right) was built in 1910. The school specialized in geological, mining, and metallurgical engineering, supplying Butte's mines with the professionals needed for advancement. Today the School of Mines is called Montana Tech, home to the Orediggers. Both the campus and its curriculum have expanded significantly, but it is still the only college in the state to offer the previous disciplines. (Then photograph courtesy of BSB Archives.)

This 1930s photograph shows a crowd watching a Montana School of Mines (now Montana Tech) Orediggers football game at the school's Leonard Field. Many of Butte's structures are constructed on top of the exposed bedrock and substantial retaining walls are common throughout its hillside neighborhoods. Leonard Field, a local project of the WPA era, still serves as the campus's hallmark entrance and is one of the greatest examples of Butte's construction feats of "man over bedrock." (Then photograph courtesy of Montana Tech Library Archives.)

The Mountain Con (short for Mountain Consolidated) underground mine closed in 1977. It holds the distinction as Butte's deepest mine, extending over 5,600 feet below the surface, as well as one of the last ones to shut down. Environmental cleanup of the mine yard and its waste rock dumps began in 2009. "Mile High, Mile Deep" is stenciled on the headframe's ore bins, in reference to Butte's elevation, the Con's depth, and probably Richard O'Malley's Butte-based novel from the 1940s. (Then photograph courtesy of Library of Congress, Historical American Engineering Record [HAER].)

The Badger State was one of Butte's steady copper producers through the first half of the 20th century. It had long been shut down when this 1970s photograph was taken. Montana Tech utilized the Badger's mine yard and entrance to the Lexington Tunnel for a short-lived underground miner-training program in the early 2000s. Compare the breadth of the Yankee Doodle Tailings Dam that spans the background in both photographs. (Then photograph courtesy of Library of Congress, HAER.)

Beginning around World War I, the Anaconda Company began the practice of using "greeting" signs to convey messages to its miners before they began their shifts. This sign from one of the underground mines in 1942 shows how the company used World War II as a means to pressure men into more productivity. A sign at the gate of the Continental Pit stresses safety more than anything else, although the current market price of copper and molybdenum are also displayed. (Then photograph courtesy of Library of Congress.)

One of the most important and respected workers in the underground mines was the hoist operator. Communicating with the miners through a series of bells and buzzes, the hoist man was responsible for raising and lowering miners to their underground locations. All of the underground mines have closed, and some are torn down, but there are still intact engine rooms or "hoist houses" that contain the roost and controls where the hoist operator did his job. (Then photograph courtesy of Library of Congress.)

"The Dry" was the locker room where miners changed clothes before and after shifts. Butte's mines were 24-hour operations, so the dry was always a lively place. The Anselmo mine, which closed in 1958, still has the name tags hanging on the lockers of the last miners who worked there. (Then photograph courtesy of World Museum of Mining.)

Underground mining is dangerous and Butte's mines were some of the deadliest in history. Over 2,500 men died in accidents underground and the perils of the profession were accepted risks, with some local businesses profiting. Butte Tombstone was one of the headstone companies in the early 1900s. Many an underground miner died when he was crushed by a large falling rock or "duggan," as they became known locally, named after a prominent local undertaker. Duggan-Dolan Mortuary still operates today. (Then photograph courtesy of BSB Archives.)

Until the Berkeley Pit shifted Butte's mining operations to the surface in 1955, hardly a week passed when there was not at least one funeral. This large public procession down Park Street was to pay respects to the 168 men who died in the Granite-Mountain Speculator disaster, an underground fire in 1917 that still stands as the worst hard rock mining accident ever. A great memorial was completed and dedicated near the site of the incident in Walkerville in 2010. (Then photograph courtesy of BSB Archives.)

The Timber Butte Mill was one of the last mining mills built in Butte (1912). The sprawling structure, constructed by copper king William Clark, was billed as a state-of-the-art mill to treat zinc ores. All that remains is a small remnant at the foot of the Timber Butte. Mills were necessary in the hard rock mining process to crush ores and treat them into concentrates, which were then ready for smelting. (Then photograph courtesy of Bob "Oxo" Corbett.)

The Butte Reduction Works (BRW) was Butte's largest historic mill and treated ores for smelting at the adjacent Colorado Smelter. Copper king William Clark owned both structures. The BRW was a primary polluter of Silver Bow Creek, channelizing it to carry away its tailings wastes. Remediation of the area in the late 1990s removed over 1 million cubic yards of waste and rebuilt the creek to a natural channel. (Then photograph courtesy of Library of Congress.)

While the majority of mineral exploration centered on the copper beneath Butte, there were a number of zinc and silver mines west of town that flourished in the late 1800s. The largest of them was the Bluebird Mine and Mill, located just east of the small town of Rocker. A few of the granite foundations of the mill overlooking Silver Bow Creek are still visible. There is a bar in Rocker called Nick's Bluebird, named after the mine. (Then photograph courtesy of BSB Archives.)

The Butte, Anaconda, & Pacific (BA&P) railroad shipped ores from all of Butte's mines to Anaconda for milling and smelting. It was nicknamed "the biggest little railroad in the world," because it hauled more tonnage daily over its 25-mile length than any other rail line. Originally envisioned to extend to the west coast, the BA&P was America's first electrified railroad. The "cow and calf" in the now photograph were exhibited at the 1915 World's Fair. (Then photograph courtesy of BSB Archives.)

The Anaconda Smelter and Reduction Works were the center of the process that turned Butte's ores into pure copper. Overlooking the city of Anaconda from the southeast, the works and smelter were an imposing sight. Completed in 1918, the stack is 585 feet tall, making it one of the largest freestanding masonry structures in the world to this day. All but the stack was dismantled after its closure in 1980. Smoke from the smelter once contaminated surrounding landscapes for miles. (Then photograph courtesy of BSB Archives.)

Butte's national significance in America's labor movement was one of the key reasons it was named a National Historic Landmark in 1961. Strikes and picket lines were commonplace and sometimes lasted for months, but strong solidarity among workers usually prevailed in better wages and working conditions. Butte still prides itself in being a union stronghold, despite the irony that the only operating mine left is non-union. This 2010 photograph shows the Plumbers Union picketing a local contractor. (Then photograph courtesy of BSB Archives.)

This 1899 photograph depicts members of Butte's Carpenters Union in front of their original hall. The hall was reconstructed in 1906 in elaborate Renaissance Revival architectural style. A testament to Butte's labor history, the new building was one of the first "labor temples" built in America and also housed the Women's Protective, Teachers, Laborers, Machinists, and Building and Construction Trades unions. The building still houses the Carpenters Union and offices at 156 West Granite Street. (Then photograph courtesy of BSB Archives.)

The early labor warfare between "the Company" and Butte Miners Union No. 1 was legendary. Industrial Workers of the World (IWW) labor organizer Frank Little was murdered in 1917, and the Union offices were bombed on more than one occasion. The one pictured here occurred in 1914, prompting the U.S. military to occupy Butte under martial law for a period to restore order. There is a historic placard and monument on North Main Street marking the site of the 1914 Miners Union bombing. (Then photograph courtesy of BSB Archives.)

In Butte's heyday, over 10,000 men worked in more than 70 individual underground mines. This historic photograph shows a miner drilling a vein for blasting. Miners, muckers, nippers, and powder monkeys were just a few of the numerous job titles men held in the underground. Open pit mining did not require most of these skilled laborers. At today's Continental Pit, ore is blasted and then loaded by an enormous electric shovel into 250-ton haul trucks. (Then photograph courtesy of Library of Congress.)

The Berkeley Pit opened in 1955, initiating the greatest change in Butte's mining history. The Pit's rapid expansion swallowed the neighborhoods of McQueen, East Side, Meaderville, and eventually, Butte's famed Columbia Gardens. Today the empty streets of McQueen are still visible, while the Pit, which closed and had its underground pumps turned off in 1982, fills with acidic, metals-laden water. There are more than 40 billion gallons, making the Berkeley the centerpiece of America's largest environmental cleanup site. (Then photograph courtesy of BSB Archives.)

The *Montana Standard's* Walter Hinick snapped this infamous photograph in the early 1960s of an Anaconda Company truck burying the Holy Savior school during the expansion of the Berkeley Pit's waste dumps. The school and the church are buried and the buildings gone, but the neighborhood streetscape of McQueen can still be made out by looking east from the deck at the Berkeley Pit viewing stand on Shields Avenue. (Then photograph courtesy of BSB Archives.)

Meaderville was a predominantly Italian-American neighborhood and the largest of Butte's burgs that were displaced in the development of the Berkeley. The Meaderville Volunteer Fire Department (VFD) produced extraordinary Christmas displays and set them up each year through the early 1950s. Butte High history teacher Chris Fisk began a service project with his classes six years ago. Students research Meaderville and the VFD's displays and rebuild them for the public to enjoy. (Photographs courtesy of Chris Fisk.)

CHAPTER 3

COMMUNITY AND CULTURE

The staggering number of state titles Butte's teams have won in nearly every sport has earned it the nickname "City of Champions." This photograph is of Butte High's 1907 football team that won the Montana and Northwest titles. Legendary daredevil Evel Knievel, Olympic skiing medalist Bryon Wilson, and professional cyclist Levi Leipheimer are notable athletes who hail from Butte. (Photograph courtesy of BSB Archives.)

This Butte highway sign, installed in the 1940s, was dismantled when local sections of I-90/I-15 were completed in the 1960s. Much of the original text was included on a new sign erected at a scenic overlook on I-15 South. Remains of the original sign's foundation can be found, peeking out from the roadside weeds along Centennial Avenue at the end of the I-90 East Walkerville exit off-ramp, but the new sign affords a much better view of the city. (Then photograph courtesy of BSB Archives.)

An early 1880s photograph looking north on Main Street near its intersection with Mercury Street shows a scene unique to any other city in the West at the same time. The streetcars are gone, and the only buildings left standing from this photograph are the small group on the left (west) side of the photograph. The Metals Bank building is the dominant building at top left. (Then photograph courtesy of BSB Archives.)

Butte's population grew lightning fast, and housing shortages were common early on. Huge boardinghouses like the Mullin House (left center of earlier photograph) on North Main Street gave meals and put a roof over miners' heads. During the busiest years, it was said the beds in the boardinghouses never went cold, as miners on different shifts would share rooms. Those days are long gone, and most of the boardinghouses, like the Mullin, no longer exist. (Then photograph courtesy of World Museum of Mining.)

There is a unique community setting in Butte, as neighborhoods sprung up around the mines out of convenience of location. This early 1940s photograph of the Anselmo Mine and its surrounding neighborhood can be closely compared to what it looks like today. The mines no longer operate, but life carries on in the shadows of the headframes. The Anselmo was a copper and zinc mine that closed in 1959. (Then photograph courtesy of BSB Archives.)

The Original Mine was closed by the time this photograph was shot on Quartz Street in the 1970s. Notice the improvements made to both buildings, as well as the environmental cleanup that has occurred since. The Original was the first mine in which copper was found (before there was a demand for it) and one of the "original" quartz lode claims on Butte Hill in the mid-1860s. (Then photograph courtesy of BSB Archives.)

The Steward was one of Butte's most productive copper and silver mines over its life of operation between 1877 and 1973. It reached a depth of just over 3,600 feet, much shallower than some of the other mines like the Anselmo (4,800), Mountain Con (5,600), and Kelley (5,000). This 1940s photograph and its modern-day pairing provide the proper perspective that many of the miner's modest homes in Butte's uptown were located literally right beneath the mines. (Then photograph courtesy of BSB Archives.)

The Courthouse Grocery in this 1970s photograph is one example of the dozens and dozens of mom-and-pop corner stores that once served Butte's neighborhoods. In the days before supermarket chains and Walmart, there was a grocery store every 10 blocks or so. All of them were out of business by the early 1990s. The Courthouse Grocery, located directly across the street from the City-County Courthouse on West Granite Street, has recently been restored but is awaiting a tenant. (Then photograph courtesy of BSB Archives.)

By the 1890s when this photograph was taken at 217 North Alabama Street, more affluent homes were commonly interspersed within the same neighborhoods of the modest miners' cottages. Class was never an issue among the hard-working residents of Butte, which is said to be the only place where the poor folk live on the hill. This Victorian-style home has lost some of its decorative adornments, but the structure remains historically intact and inhabited. (Then photograph courtesy of BSB Archives.)

A pair of finely clothed gentlemen survey Butte looking east from a boardwalk on Copper Street in this photograph taken around 1910. Though a western mining town, Butte folks preferred to dress more distinguished than the standard Montana cowboy, and this photograph was taken at the height of Butte's affluence. The building on the central horizon in both photographs is the federal courthouse on North Main Street, now named to honor one of Butte's most famous politicians, Sen. Mike Mansfield. (Then photograph courtesy of BSB Archives.)

By the early 1890s, Butte was producing more copper than any single place on the planet, and the resulting wealth accumulated by successful mine and business owners was manifested in magnificent architecture like this Victorian mansion of the era on North Main Street. Located directly across the street from the Steward Mine, this early structure has been preserved immaculately over the 40-year-span between these two photographs and remains one of the historic district's sparkling gems. (Then photograph courtesy of BSB Archives.)

Butte's cosmopolitan population demanded everything America's largest cities enjoyed, including entertainment. Through the 1950s, a number of theaters and opera houses served the mining city, including the American, the Rialto, the Broadway, and the Temple Theatre, as it appeared in this 1930s photograph. Over the years, all either burned or were demolished. Built by the Masons in 1923, the Temple (now the Mother Lode) was restored to its early Beaux-Arts glory and reopened as an upscale theater in 2000. (Then photograph courtesy of BSB Archives.)

William Clark established the Columbia Gardens in 1899 to provide a bright spot for Butte residents to recreate and escape the industrial town's smoke and filth. As Butte's "crown jewel," the gardens were located a short trolley ride east of town and offered a lake, amusement park with roller coaster, playgrounds, pavilion, and a gorgeous botanical center with thousands of plants. The gardens closed on Labor Day 1973 and mysteriously burned that November, perhaps the greatest casualty of the Berkeley Pit. (Then photograph courtesy of World Museum of Mining.)

Marcus Daly was an avid fan of horse racing and built opulent facilities in Butte and Anaconda before his death in 1900. Butte's track was located off the hill where horses could run on a flat surface. The neighborhood and volunteer fire department still bear the racetrack name, and the site of the former track is on the grounds of East Middle School and Bulldog Memorial Stadium where the local high school teams host football games and track meets. (Then photograph courtesy of BSB Archives.)

St. Johns Episcopal was one of Butte's first churches in 1881. The church expanded a number of times at the same location, the last of which occurred after a fire ravaged the building in 1921. This historic photograph was taken prior to the 1919 fire, probably around 1900. The post-fire addition of the square turrets to the building's front emphasizes the Norman architectural style prevalent in many Episcopal structures. The church is still open at 15 North Idaho Street. (Then photograph courtesy of BSB Archives.)

Butte has always harbored a great population of Irish Catholics, explaining why its St. Patrick's Day celebration is tops in the region. There were once nearly as many Catholic schools as there were public. The Montana bishop laid the cornerstone of the new boys' Butte Central Catholic High School erected in 1924 at the corner of Idaho and Mercury Streets. Butte Central High is now located a block to the north, and the old building houses Butte's Small Business Development Center. (Then photograph courtesy of BSB Archives.)

The Trinity United Methodist Church was another of Butte's early churches. Located at the top of North Main Street just before entering Walkerville, it was built in the 1890s. The church has not changed much at all—a salute to its tedious maintenance and upkeep. (Then photograph courtesy of BSB Archives.)

This pre-1906 photograph looks east down Park Street and captures Butte's early metropolitan character. On the right, the steel framing is visible that would become the Metals Bank, one of Butte's tallest and longest-standing major buildings. Financed by copper king Augustus Heinze for $325,000, it was designed by architect Cass Gilbert, who also created New York City's Woolworth building and the U.S. Supreme Court building in Washington, D.C. Today the building houses a restaurant, bar, casino, and apartments. (Then photograph courtesy of BSB Archives.)

Butte boomed during America's immigration peak. Citizens came from the globe's four corners, so to speak. Diverse ethnicities occupied distinct neighborhoods, like the Irish (Dublin Gulch) and Italian (Meaderville). Butte also had a Chinatown, now home to the Mai Wah Society, a Chinese-American heritage nonprofit housed in the historic Mai Wah Noodle Parlor/Wai Chong Tai mercantile building. Today Danny Wong and wife Sharon Tam still operate the Pekin Noodle Parlor, a unique Butte restaurant two buildings away on Main Street. (Then photograph courtesy of BSB Archives.)

The Parisian House was built in 1890 to house the Parisian Dye Works, a textile and linen company. It was located on the western edge of the red light district and much of its business was generated from the prostitutes of the numerous brothels. Today the building serves as Butte's uptown post office on the southeast corner of Galena and Dakota Streets. The St. Francis Apartments, located on the right, were built in 1912. (Then photograph courtesy of BSB Archives.)

This 1970 photograph shows the Copper Block on the corner of Galena and Wyoming Streets. Built in 1892, it was the headquarters of Butte's famous red light district, once home to over 1,000 working ladies, who played a significant role in the town's formative culture. The Dumas was the last brothel to close in 1982. The Copper Block was torn down in 1992. An interpretive park adorned with metal silhouettes of the former "ladies of the night" marks its place. (Then photograph courtesy of BSB Archives.)

The passage of the Volstead Act in 1919 marked a big change in the way Butte's hard-working/hard-drinking population would cope. This prohibition-era photograph depicts U.S. troops draining liquor into the storm drain in front of a bar on East Second Street. Many of Butte's bars became "cigar stores" to appear legitimate, and underground speakeasies were common throughout the 1920s. Today there are more than 100 drinking establishments in town, including the Scoop, one of Butte's last neighborhood taverns. (Then photograph courtesy of BSB Archives.)

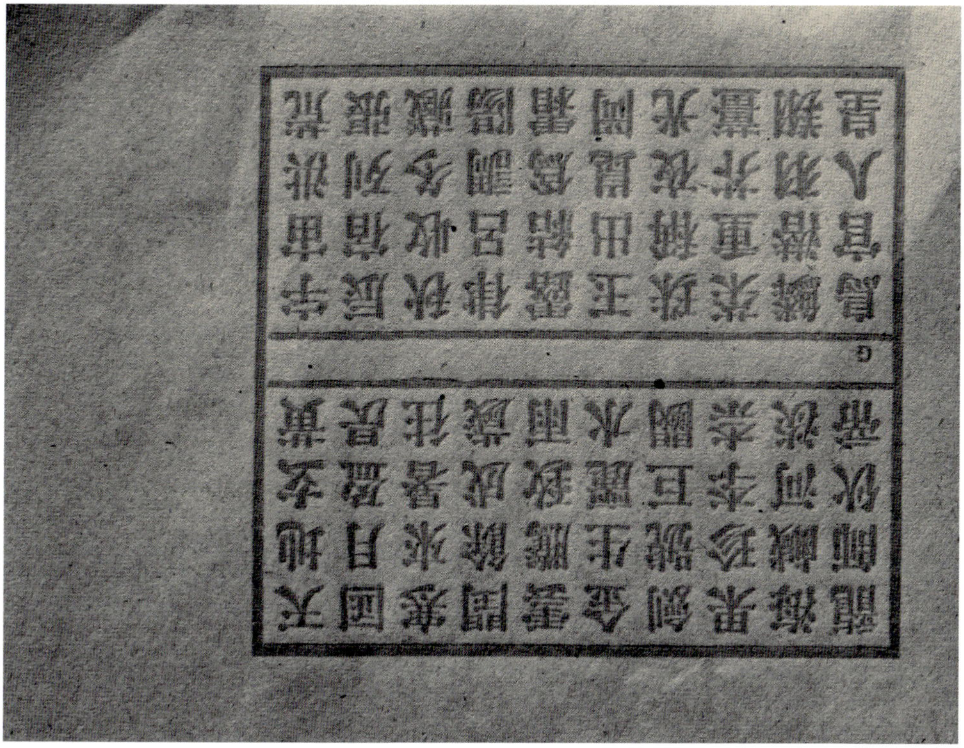

Butte is credited with creating the gambling game Keno. Before World War I, a number of gambling parlors in Butte's Chinatown ran an ancient Chinese lotto game in which players would choose 10 Chinese characters from a card of 80, as shown on a 1910 card from a parlor at 119 South Main Street. In 1935, when Nevada legalized gambling, Frances Lyden of Butte's Crown Cigar Store took the game to Reno, replacing the characters with numbers, giving birth to America's first Keno. (1910 Chinese Lotto card courtesy of Danny Wong Tam.)

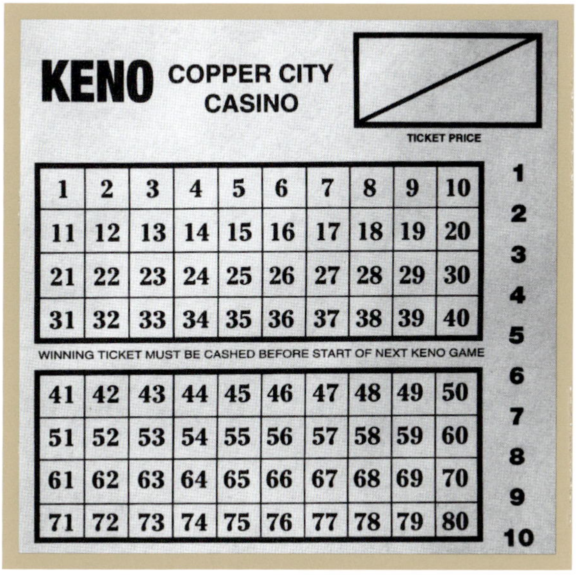

KENO COPPER CITY CASINO

TICKET PRICE

1	2	3	4	5	6	7	8	9	10
11	12	13	14	15	16	17	18	19	20
21	22	23	24	25	26	27	28	29	30
31	32	33	34	35	36	37	38	39	40

WINNING TICKET MUST BE CASHED BEFORE START OF NEXT KENO GAME

41	42	43	44	45	46	47	48	49	50
51	52	53	54	55	56	57	58	59	60
61	62	63	64	65	66	67	68	69	70
71	72	73	74	75	76	77	78	79	80

1 2 3 4 5 6 7 8 9 10

This 1940s night scene paints a great picture of Butte's neon-lit, uptown center at Park and Main Streets. The M&M Cigar Store, the circular sign at left, started business in 1892 and remained open 24 hours a day, seven days a week, as a bar, restaurant, and gambling hall until its closure in 2004. Today a number of Butte's uptown businesses, like the Metals Bank (largest building) are beginning to thrive again in what hopefully will become a historic uptown renaissance. (Then photograph courtesy of BSB Archives.)

Another of Butte's busy streets is Montana Street. This *c.* 1920 view looks north across intersections with Park, Broadway, and Granite. A number of major buildings from Butte's zenith as a metropolitan area have perished over the years, like the Montana Theatre (middle left), which burned in the 1950s. Notice the ghost sign for Lutey's on the Stephens Block building (right) still remains. Lutey's was a successful grocery early on, with several locations, before going out of business in 1924. (Then photograph courtesy of BSB Archives.)

Butte has always loved a parade. This 1930s Fourth of July parade on Broadway captures one of the floats, as well as two of uptown's prominent buildings: the Hirbour Tower (on right) and the First National Bank, established 1877. The eight-story Hirbour was touted as Butte's first "skyscraper" in 1901, using the same construction methods as the first high-rises built in Chicago. Today the bank houses an engineering firm and the Hirbour's ground floor is a women's boutique, Kally's Korner. (Then photograph courtesy of BSB Archives.)

Butte's most prosperous years leading up to World War I were an era of great construction and consumption. This 1910 photograph of Pioneer Fuel and Brick Company on Maryland Avenue gives an idea of how much coal and building materials went into creating "Montana's only metropolis," as Butte was dubbed on an early postcard. The frenzy settled in the 1920s, but Pioneer Concrete, which also fabricated pumice building blocks as recently as the early 2000s, still does business at the same location. (Then photograph courtesy of BSB Archives.)

Located at the convergence of railroad spurs in the east central part of town, the Warehouse District was a busy place when Butte prospered. This 1907 photograph of Henningsen Produce at 740 South Wyoming Street depicts the fancy architecture characteristic of even the warehouses. Recent fires have leveled some of the district's buildings, but the ones that still stand, albeit many of them vacant, remain an imposing remembrance of the Mining City's demand for goods during its heyday. (Then photograph courtesy of BSB Archives.)

Butte's last commercial district to develop was Harrison Avenue on the south end of town. Harrison did not have the impressive architecture of the uptown, as it was developed during Butte's economic decline post–World War I. A notable business in this 1950s photograph is Grant's Fly Shop (next to the barbershop), owned by legendary fly tier and conservationist George Grant. Today Harrison serves as Butte's primary commercial area, although a few early structures remain intact. (Then photograph courtesy of BSB Archives.)

All of the buildings and structures in the Butte-Anaconda historic landmark district are not in pristine condition, as this photograph of the old Soroptomists' Home on West Quartz Street attests. Once a thriving refuge for Butte's orphans through the Depression and World Wars I and II, the Soroptomist building has fallen into disrepair and awaits full restoration. Many of the district's buildings are in similar condition or worse, while some have been demolished. More recently, preservation and restoration are gaining significant ground. (Then photograph courtesy of BSB Archives.)

CHAPTER 4

Restoration, Revitalization, and Preservation

The Anaconda–Deer Lodge City-County Courthouse is one of the premiere historic public buildings in the state. Constructed in 1890 and designed by architects Bell and Kent, the spectacular building is undergoing the first phase of a $2 million restoration. Restoration—both architectural and ecological—is both prevalent and necessary throughout the Butte-Anaconda National Historic Landmark District.

The intersection of Park and Main Streets is arguably the heart of Butte's Uptown District and historically, the busiest part of town. Even though most of Butte's present day-to-day business takes place on the Flats, or southern part of town, when a resident boldly proclaims they will "kiss your ass" in a high-visibility public place, the location is still "on the corner of Park and Main." (Then photograph courtesy of BSB Archives.)

The Montana Hotel, built by Marcus Daly in 1889, stands central in Anaconda's historic district. The Montana was once considered a luxury hotel of the West, but the ornate masonry structure had fallen vacant and into decay by the 1970s. Much like Butte, Anaconda is finding a new lease on economic life, billing itself as the place "where Main Street meets the mountains." The Montana is alive again with a Subway and a number of professional offices. (Then photograph courtesy of Library of Congress.)

Butte was the largest city between Minneapolis and Spokane in the early 1900s, making it a major stop for all of the western railroads for freight and passengers. The Milwaukee Railroad constructed this elegant station in 1916 to primarily serve its Chicago, Milwaukee, and St. Paul passenger trains. Local television station KXLF has called the building home since 1957. When the station was renovated in the 1970s, the project was billed as the city's first major building restoration project. (Then courtesy of BSB Archives.)

This late 1970s photograph shows the former state of the Butte–Silver Bow Public Archives building. Constructed in 1900, the building was the former home of Butte's fire department headquarters. Butte values its history as much as any other place. A voter-approved $8 million bond restored and expanded the historic quarters to a beautiful, state-of-the-art archival facility in 2010. Components of the restoration, such as the centerpiece ornament on the former fire department, were incorporated with accurate attention to historic detail. (Then photograph courtesy of BSB Archives.)

The Owsley Block was built in 1889 by a former Butte mayor and housed a number of businesses, including the Hoffman Hotel and Newman's Bootery, before falling vacant in the 1990s. From the time the first photograph was taken in 1970, the building was restored by its current owner and is now the home of Trimbo's Off-the-Hook Pizza. Travel Channel's Adam Richman tackled Trimbo's 5-pound stromboli in a 2010 episode of the popular television show *Man v. Food*. (Then photograph courtesy of BSB Archives.)

Arthur Mueller, president of the former Centennial Brewing Company, built this beautiful Queen Anne–style mansion in 1895 at the corner of Park and Alabama Streets. A number of mansions from this era on West Park Street have been immaculately preserved through the years by a number of owners. The former Mueller home—for sale in this 2010 photograph—is a good representative of some of the more ostentatious architecture found in many of Butte's early upscale homes. (Then photograph courtesy of BSB Archives.)

Butte's thirsty population was served by several breweries before Prohibition. As seen here in the 1920s, one of the originals, the Butte Brewing Company, emerged from the Prohibition era as the strongest survivor of its counterparts. Butte Beer ghost signs still remind Butte drinkers "your hometown product deserves preference." Chuck and Lyza Schnabel opened the Quarry Brewery in an old automotive garage at 45 West Galena Street in 2006, ending Butte's dry spell without a local brewery since the 1960s. (Then photograph courtesy of BSB Archives.)

Thompson Park was established by an act of Congress in 1917 to provide outdoor recreation opportunities for Butte's residents. At over 3,500 acres, it is one of the largest municipal parks in the United States, more than three times as large as New York City's Central Park. Thompson Park is jointly owned and operated by Butte–Silver Bow and the U.S. Forest Service. A $1.5 million-restoration of the park facilities and ecosystem improvements are ongoing. (Then photograph courtesy of World Museum of Mining.)

Built in the early 1880s, the Old Works was the first smelting facility in Anaconda. By the 1980s, Anaconda was named a federal Superfund site, and the Old Works was a collection of crumbling masonry foundations and millions of tons of toxic wastes. An innovative cleanup in the 1990s resulted in Montana's only Jack Nicklaus–designed golf course. Sand traps on the course are filled with black slag dust, and many of the old decaying structures are incorporated into the links. (Then photograph courtesy of BSB Archives.)

Over a century of mega-mining and smelting without any significant environmental regulations created a mess of legendary proportions. Butte and Anaconda's legacy of contamination extend 120 miles down the Upper Clark Fork watershed, making it America's largest complex of federal cleanup sites. This photograph pair of the Lexington Mine in Walkerville shows how many of the old dumps were capped and revegetated in the mid-1980s through the 1990s. There are thousands of acres requiring remedy in the former mining corridor. (Then photograph courtesy of EPA.)

The Bell Diamond, erected in the early 1900s, was Butte's first big headframe. When the underground closed in the 1970s, surface yards were left as-is, creating an archaeologically significant industrial landscape. They were also toxic. Recent reclamation of historic wastes not only aims to minimize health impacts, but also to provide reuse, like the walking trail in this 2010 photograph. The Bell Diamond is part of the Granite Mountain Memorial Interpretive Area, located northeast of town. (Then photograph courtesy of Library of Congress.)

Another of Butte's headframes still standing is the Belmont. This comparison shows a good representation of the East Butte Revitalization Project, an effort to revitalize the town's most blighted area. The project began in 2000 with the reclamation and reuse of the Belmont. In addition to standard reclamation, the mine's engine room was retrofitted to house Butte's Senior Citizen Center. Another new building is the Maroon Activity Center, a multi-events and athletic arena constructed in 2004 by Butte Central. (Then photograph courtesy of BSB Archives.)

Beginning in the mid-1860s and continuing through most of the 1990s, Silver Bow Creek was largely devoid of any life, historically serving as a conduit for Butte's mining and municipal wastes. This photograph pair shows the creek just before ecological restoration began in 1998 and what it looks like now since its cleanup. The price tag for restoration of the creek's 23-mile length is $85 million, anticipated for completion in 2012. (Both courtesy of Natural Resource Damage Program.)

All of Butte's restoration is not environmental, bricks, and mortar. A 1915 Labor Day parade passes down West Park Street in front of the Montana Bakery, housed in the Haller Building. Today the building is home to the Hummingbird Café, a popular organic food and coffee house, and Sacred Ground, a space where new age speakers and yoga classes are held. (Then photograph courtesy of Hummingbird Café.)

Butte's newest title is "The Festival City," because of its success hosting celebrations like St. Patrick's Day and most recently, the 70th through 72nd National Folk Festival. Over 300,000 attended the cultural event over the years Butte hosted it. The Original Mine was the main stage, drawing great crowds over the three-day event held each July from 2008 to 2010. The crowd in this 2010 photograph is larger than any gathering ever seen at the Original Mine, including its busiest years of labor. (Original/Folk Festival; Then photograph courtesy of BSB Archives.)

A 1914 gathering of the Butte Motorcycle Club on Park Street exhibits the town's sophisticated nature early on when most frontier towns were still riding horses and wagons. Butte becomes an exclusive motorcycle town the last weekend in July each year when it hosts Evel Knievel Days, a celebration held to honor its most famous son. The 10th annual festival for the late, world-famous stuntman is in 2011. The event draws tens of thousands to Butte's uptown streets and businesses. (Then photograph courtesy of BSB Archives.)

Mining and smelting are integral to Butte and Anaconda's culture. The Anaconda smelter appears in a stained glass window of St. Peter's Catholic Church, built in 1904 on the corner of Alder and Fourth Streets in Anaconda. The head frames synonymous with Butte's underground mining appear regularly in signs and logos. This sign made of granite is a recent example, erected for a Butte correctional facility located on East Mercury Street in 2009.

The sun has set on Butte's days as an industrial metropolis. Gone are the cloudy days of the early 1900s when environment sat painfully behind America's speeding progress. The sky is blue, the waters run much clearer, and places like the Butte Reduction Works that churned out copper day and night are gone . . . almost. This poignant shot of Silver Bow Creek confined by slag walls captures Butte's future as a place where the past will always be cherished and the costs never forgotten. (Then photograph courtesy of Atlantic Richfield Corporation.)

Consistent with our mission to preserve history on a local level, this book was printed in South Carolina on American-made paper and manufactured entirely in the United States. Products carrying the accredited Forest Stewardship Council (FSC) label are printed on 100 percent FSC-certified paper.

MADE IN THE USA